Volcano Mountain at Cotopaxi was named by Henry Thomas who discovered the mine in the gulch to the North.

WESTERN FREMONT COUNTY COLORADO

This is the forgotten area in historical research. The comings and goings of all the important people and the history of important places in Colorado usually skips over the fact that the Upper Arkansas River was a major player in transportation and economic development.

This book is a tribute to the many pioneers who came into the beautiful Canyon of the Arkansas and eventually homesteaded or developed a business that served the outside world on its way to the riches of the gold mines or rode the railroad into fame. Cmc

THE LAND BEYOND THE GORGE

The story of the western part of Fremont County, Colorado told through pictures and remembrances.

by Carol McNew

LEAVING CIVILIZATION BEHIND

OLD STAGE ROADS FROM CANON CITY

The stagecoach and freight routes in pre 1875 are depicted in a fascinating map drawn by a gentleman working for the Bureau of Land Management in 1975. It shows the various routes which the freighters and miners took to go from Canon City to the mines in Leadville, Breckenridge, Fairplay, Westcliffe, Rosita and Cripple Creek.

The interesting thing about this map and the region of Western Fremont County is that most of the routes which were then "main" roads are still used today as county highways.

When Highway 50 was cut through the river canyon, it shortened the route considerably. Mileage had been calculated from the villages in the Western part of the County, across country, following creeks and divides. There is a document showing mileage to Canon City from Texas Creek as 37 miles.

The routes were primitive and dangerous to travel. The lure of the gold and other riches to be gained in the mines were a powerful incentive for folks to jump on the 6 horse stagecoach, The team had to be split to go around some of the corners and the "shelf" character of the road was a factor in trying to pass another vehicle. There are no statistics to show how many folks were killed or injured on the highways at that time.

The fathers and founders of Cañon City were well on their way to civilizing the citizens of that city by the time the transportation promoters were enticed into the Cañon City to Leadville route.

The freighters and stagecoach operators had been hauling produce, mine and smelter parts and other requirements for the blossoming economies of the upper Arkansas River enterprises. The railroad was a few steps behind but realized that there was money to be made going up and coming down. Loads of ore went down to smelters; the necessities of daily life not produced at the mining towns were hauled back up to the burgeoning communities of Leadville, Aspen, Breckenridge, Fairplay, Alma and many more.

Railroad ties and charcoal for the smelters and mills were a major product of the areas along the river. Ties were floated down the river during flood, and the charcoal burners which graced every small community burned thousands of tons of piñon wood which was cut and hauled to the kilns by industrious pioneers.

The denuded hills and valleys were then put to use as hay and grain meadows as well as pasture for the burgeoning cattle industry.

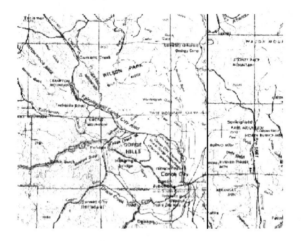

This map is a depiction of the stage and freight roads to the mines and towns west of Canon City. The map was produced under the auspices of the Department of Interior, Bureau of Land Management by Glen R. Scott in 1975, map #I-930. Thanks to the USGS for its use.

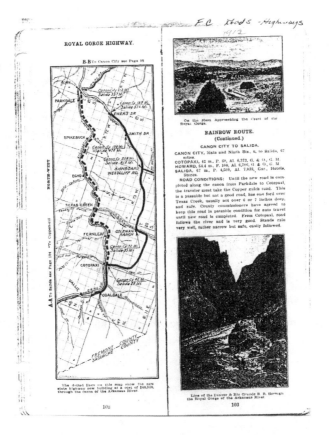

The Rainbow Route into the Grand Canyon of the Arkansas River in 1912 was a fantastic dream, the old road as above.

Parkdale bridge – crossing the Arkansas River as it enters the Royal Gorge

INTO THE CANYON OF THE ARKANSAS RIVER

U.S. Highway 50 enters the canyon of the upper Arkansas River after circling the mighty Royal Gorge. The Highway is a "recent" addition as far as the history of the area. The road from Parkdale to Texas Creek was completed in 1920, a dirt, one lane, and very treacherous stretch of highway.

The first settlement is Parkdale, which sits astride the river, with store, school and post office on one side, and the Railroad Station and residences on the other. The bridge, which crosses to the north side, is known by the name of the ranchers who owned the land, the Harveys.

The highway was built when most of the machinery was horse-drawn and workers did a lot of pick and shovel work. When you observe some of the sheer cliffs that were blown to accommodate the roadway, you will appreciate the tremendous cost in labor.

It has been noted that the river canyon has been transformed by the railroad on one side, and the highway on the other.

Parkdale in the above photo before the Highway 50 project began in 1912. Notice the large monolithic boulder just as the road crosses the river. The new look at Parkdale, t(top of next page) road crosses the railroad tracks just north of the river.. The Royal Gorge Route train now runs on these tracks, as well as the gravel from a pit that has been developed where the old ranch house sits in Left distance.

The silo and concrete buildings are the feldspar processing plant which has been out of business for 40 years.

The construction of Highway 50, The Rainbow Route was aided by the convict road gangs that did a great deal of the work.

The trails and roads that approached Cañon City from the West all had to circumvent the huge gash in the earth they called the Gorge. When the bridge was constructed in 1930, the name became the Royal Gorge, and the attraction has been visited by millions of people over the last 80 years. The 80th birthday was in 2010.

Prison Road Camp while building Highway 50 along the Arkansas River

The Colorado Department of Corrections was a mighty force in many of the building projects throughout Fremont County from the 1880's through the late 1970's. You will notice as you drive along Highway 50 through Big Horn Sheep Canyon that there are old road beds to the South of the present roadway, and they have been buttressed with rock work. This is all indicative of the prison labor.

There are also many bridges that were built by the WPA workers during the depression years as well.

The bridge abutment at Five Points Campground where there was a bridge across the river from the Railroad track to service an Assayer on the South side, and his mining products.

SPIKEBUCK, ECHO, FIVEPOINTS AND PINNACLE ROCK

The railroad named many of the places along the river as it climbed its way to the West from Cañon City. The Grand Canyon of the Arkansas was a challenge to the designers and engineers of the roadbed, and a man-killer for the section crews and construction gangs.

The railroad leaves Parkdale and immediately is squeezed into the canyon by steep granite outcroppings and boulders the size of houses. The first really wide place in the road was an area named Spikebuck, where forts were manned during the railroad war. Today, this area has been developed into a boat landing with restrooms and tables for picnics. The fisherman are welcomed here as well.

Around a couple of curves on towards the west is the area called Five Points which also was defendable by forts and hide-outs of the railroad roustabouts and hired guards who were charged with keeping the railroad interests defended. They built rock forts on the steep hillsides as vantage points to protect the railroad construction gangs working below.

Echo Canyon Tunnel, on Rainbow Route after construction in 1930.

ECHO CANYON

The tunnels blasted into the rock at the Echo Curve were a testimony to the per-severance of the road builder's grit. The tunnels were removed in later years as the road was expanded and widened, but at this particular place, the curves are still treacherous.

PINNACLE ROCK

The distinctive shape of this formation is a great goad to the imagination. If you ask three different people what it represents to them, you will get three different answers. The Bureau of Land Management has improved the area directly below the rock next to the Arkansas River, and it is now a boat ramp, picnic area, fishing spot and viewing area for Bighorn Sheep.

There are restrooms available, and the turn-off is more convenient now since they have turning lanes from both East and West. The rock is 3 miles East of Texas Creek.

Texas Creek Depot, one of several building that existed for many years on the north side of the river along the railroad tracks.

QUICK FACTS:

The nature of the Rocky Mountain vastness lends itself to visions of lonesome and reclusive men. However, that scene vanished into the past with the coming of settlers and industry. They were no longer needed to guide explorers across the wilderness, nor were there very many herds of buffalo or beaver in the streams.

The cowboy moved onto the scene with the advent of the cattle barons and ranchers who used the government ground as their own, some to the tune of thousands of acres for free grazing. The cowboys were required to watch over, round-up in the spring and fall and generally manage the mighty herds that wandered at will throughout the hills and valleys of the upper country.

When the government opened the public land to homesteading, a river of people came into the West Fremont area to take up their

160 acres, or more, for five years. After "Proving up", the land was theirs to do with as they wished. The Land Office in Pueblo was the official registrar of these homesteads, and the documents produced from the filings are a treasure to read. The documents stating official ownership gave many people the start they needed in life to either continue as ranchers or farmers, or to sell and make a profit, allowing them to go on to other enterprises. The ranchers dubbed the homesteaders "nesters", and a small community of 15 to 20 homesteaders was formed north of Cotopaxi and named "Nesterville".

For several years Texas Creek was the only post office in the west end of Fremont County and everyone got his mail there. Just when it or the others were established, is not known but we found letters bearing the date of 1876 addressed to Texas Creek. One of these was a post card to Louis Muhlbach, mailed July 1876. It was mailed from Rosita by the County Superintendent of schools. The very early settlers must have gone to Canon City for their mail.

Coaldale has had several names since its beginning. In 1880 letters were addressed to it under the name of Hayden. In 1882 it was going under the name of Palmer. Why this change was made is not known. The name Palmer was retained until 1884 at least, and then it changed to Hendricks. The probable reason for this was the confusing of it with Palmer Lake in the delivery of mail. We do not know when nor why it was changed to Coaldale. It was, however after 1890 as at that time letters were still addressed to Hendricks.

Howard was named for the family of Howards who were early settlers there.

The Hillside store and post office were first built near the Squires place, down Texas Creek from the present site of Hillside. They were built by a man named Brown, and were built on the side of the hill—hence, the name Hillside. Later both were moved to the present site, but the name was retained.

In the opinion of the most people in Cotopaxi it was named by the railroad about 1890. What town there was before that seems not to have had a name. Some say it is an Indian word meaning "burning mound"; others believe it means "narrow pass", and still others say it means "lost trail".

The first school district organized in this section was the Stout

Creek school in 1873. The school was located on Hamilton Creek near the Joe Lamb Rock. There were four or five pupils. It was a log school house and there was a foot bridge across the river to the school house. The teacher was Mrs. Adams.

The village of Cotopaxi as it looked in 1906. The wooden truss bridge was the first of many. The present bridge is a two lane, modern bridge that accommodates the traffic that is now present.

The school is located one quarter mile north of Highway 50 on County Road 12, and is a modern structure, expanded year by year to fit the student body. The graduating classes usually are no more than 30 students.

The Creek that empties into the Arkansas River at Cotopaxi is Bernard's Creek.

HISTORY OF THE WEST END OF FREMONT COUNTY*

We are indebted to the following people for the information on the early settlers of this part of Fremont County: Mrs. Cora McCrory, Mr. and Mrs. Guy Benton, Mr. Charlie Smith, Mrs. E.C. McCormick, Mrs. L. L. Froman, Mrs. Mary Hayden, Mr. and Mrs. Bert Blackford, Mrs. Coleman, Mrs. R. D. Baker, Mr. George Cooper, Mr. and Mrs. Charlie McCoy, Mrs. Denick, Miss Cora Lamb, Mr. Frank Lamb, and Mr. T. Lee Witcher.

The west end of Fremont County was first occupied by three major Indian tribes: The Utes, Arapahoes and Cheyenne. The Utes finally drove the others out. It was a favorite hunting ground for all three tribes. By the time the first settlers came, the trouble between the tribes had been settled, and for the most part, the Indians were peaceful. Two Indian scares, however, were given to the early white people of this vicinity. Neither was from the Indians around here, but came from rumor of trouble or trouble some place else. The first of these scares was caused by the rumor that Indians had burned Saguache, in the San Luis Valley, and were on their way across the mountains by way of Hayden Pass to massacre the people in the Arkansas Valley.

The people of the east end of Pleasant Valley (now known as Coaldale) gathered the women and children into one house. About forty of them spent the night there while the men spent it lying on Hayden pass waiting for the Indians. There seems never to have been anything more to this uprising than just rumor.

The second scare was at the time of the Meeker Massacre in Western Colorado. A warning came to citizens here that they had better be prepared for an Indian attack, for supposedly the Indians had killed all whites at Meeker, were coming east down the Arkansas. That uprising was stopped at the beginning and so nothing more came of it; but many people not having any way to get out, hid out in the brush.

The Indians did not make homes here, but used the country mostly as they traveled through. They wintered south and east of Canon City and spent the summers in the San Luis Valley and places on the Western Slope.

The Indian trails through this part of Fremont County were followed by the early roads. These trails were made by the Indians to be used by their horses. They tied a pole to either side of the horse, letting the ends drag on the ground. Between these poles they hung hammock-like a piece of Buckskin on which were placed their belongings. These poles dragging on the ground wore the trail deep into the earth. "Thus", say the pioneers, "were worn the first highways of this country."

The main trail followed by most of the Indians came up the Arkansas river past Canon City to Grape Creek, up Grape Creek and across to Copper Gulch. From Copper Gulch it went across Indian Springs park to Texas Creek. (This refers to the creek and not the station on the railroad.) From the creek, the trail went across the hills and through the brush and timber past the place where Pete Young now lives on Oak Creek three miles south of Cotopaxi, up the gulch to the west of that place and across the divide into Cottonwood Creek. Near what we know as Coaldale, the trails forked. One of them led over Hayden Pass into the San Luis Valley; the other followed the hills at the foot of the Sangre de Cristos towards Salida. Because of the narrowness of the canyon, a direct route by the river was impossible. The road built for stage coaches and freight wagons followed this same route.

At the time when the country was first settled by the white people, the famous Ouray was chief of the Utes. Probably to him is due the friendly attitude of the Indians. Some of the early settlers knew this chief personally. William Stout was among this number. A nephew of the famous chief was killed on the old Davis Place at Howard, when he was riding a bucking horse. He is buried at Howard. An early Indian camp was located near the foot of Baldy Mountain. It was here and in other similar camps that the white people became acquainted with the camp customs of the Indians. They lived in a form of tent made by throwing buffalo or deer skins over lodge poles; after the white man came in, bringing canvas with them, the Indians made use of it for this purpose.

They made bread of flour and water without any shortening. This, after the arrival of the whites, was mixed in the top of the sack of flour. The bread was baked in little cakes on huge flat stones heated by a fire. The Indian continued to spit upon the stone to see when it was hot enough for the bread. Above this was hung a piece of meat to cook; as it cooked the grease and juices were allowed to drip down on to the bread. This provided both shortening and flavoring for the bread.

The Indians, in going through the country always did a lot of begging from the white settlers. One day some time after a group of Indians had gone through the section near Howard, a woman carrying a newborn baby appeared at the door of one of the pioneer homes. She had been left by the group alone to care for her baby; it was assumed by them that she would catch up and be in camp that night.

It was shortly after the white people came here that the camp near Baldy Mountain was abandoned. One night amid a great deal of confusion, the sound of drums and wailing was heard in the Indian camp. The next morning very early they all left, walking Indian file across the hills and onto the East. The white people thought that perhaps the chief of the tribe had died and they went to the camp to see if they could find a reason for the excitement of the night before. However, they could find no signs of a grave or anything else to show why they had left. The Indians were never known to use that camp again.

The pioneers lived in log cabins, and most of their furniture was made by the men themselves and consisted mainly of benches, a rude table and a stove. The pioneers of this section had stoves and did not use fireplaces for cooking. One family had an organ. Shortly after coming to Colorado, W. K. Eggleston bought an old-fashioned organ, better known as the melodian. This proved to be of much interest to one of the Indian chiefs who stopped at the house one day. He was very much impressed as he watched Mrs. Eggleston playing and pumping the organ. He watched for a while and then suddenly left. Although the Indians were peaceful, any unusual or sudden movements aroused the suspicions of the whites. For a while the family was worried about what he meant, but he soon returned with several squaws. After he came in with them, he insisted that Mrs. Eggleston should pump the organ. When she finally complied with his wishes, he got one of the squaws to touch the keys. This sudden and unusual noise frightened the squaws greatly. The old chief became so amused that he rolled on the floor laughing.

The section of Fremont County and the surrounding counties between Canon City and Salida, Westcliffe and north of the river for several miles, because of its inaccessibility, was one of the last sections of the state to be settled by white people. People had settled in the eastern part of Fremont County, the Wet Mountain Valley, the San Luis Valley and in the Cottonwood country, a number of years before this section was reached.

One of the first white men to go through this country and also one of our first settlers, was Joseph Lamb. "Joe" Lamb was born in North Carolina in 1836. At a very early age he left for the West. He was one of the first mail carriers in the Kansas Territory, as Colorado was then called. He carried the first mail from Denver to California Gulch near where Leadville now stands. This trip was made on snow shoes. He also took part in the Battle of Sand Creek near Lamar. It was at this battle that he got the Indian scalp which is still in possession of the Lamb family.

During the early 1860's there was a group of Mexican outlaws, the Espinosa's, who terrorized the upper part of the Arkansas Valley. They held up stage coaches, robbed and murdered. There are many stories connected with them. Some say the number of their victims reached seventy-two; some say they robbed and stole only enough to live on. In any case it seems their motive was revenge. During the winter of 1862-1863 a posse was organized to capture—dead or alive—these outlaws. Joe Lamb was a member of this posse. Near Howard is a rock known as the Joe Lamb rock where he is supposed to have lain in wait for the Espinosa's.

The posse caught up with the robbers in the Pikes peak country, north of Canon City. It was here that Lamb shot and killed one of them. The other two escaped and were later killed by Tom Tobin, a famous Indian scout, near Fort Garland. There was a large reward offered by the government for the capture or the killing of the three men, but for some reason it was never paid.

Freighting by burro from Canon City to Leadville was Lamb's next venture. It was in 1870 he took up a homestead on Texas Creek; this is now the Coleman Ranch. (Rosenthal, 1995*)

There were settlers in Pleasant Valley before there were any around Cotopaxi. Pleasant Valley was the name given to the valley which now includes the Howard and Coaldale communities. The first families moved in there in 1870, 71, 72. The first two families in Howard were Jonah Perroguine and William Stout; and the first two in Coaldale were Louis Muhlbach and the Haydens.

William Stout came to Colorado from Tennessee. He came into Pleasant Valley by way of South Park in April, 1872 with his wife, three children, and one team of oxen, one team of horses and thirty-six cents. He took up a place two miles this side of Howard which is still known as the Stout Place. Mrs. Cora McCrory, his daughter was the first white child born in Howard.

The Hayden family came to Colorado from Iowa, and lived in Bijou Basin northeast of Colorado Springs for a while. In 1870 or 71 they came to Pleasant Valley. Hayden Creek, south of Coaldale, was named for Mr. Hayden, but the pass was named later for a surveyor by the same name who surveyed it for the government.

Louis Muhlbach left Chicago after the famous Chicago fire in 1871, and came to Pleasant Valley by way of Pueblo. In 1872 he homesteaded the place on which his daughter, Mrs. Guy Benton, of Coaldale now lives. (4 mi. So. Hayden Creek*). Mr. Muhlbach was a naturalized citizen in 1867. Mr. Muhlbach was one of the first, if not the first, county commissioner from the west end of the county. He was commissioner in 1882.

W. K. Eggleston left Iowa in 1872 and came to Colorado Springs on the railroad. From there the family came by ox teams to make their new home three miles south of Cotopaxi. They had to cut a road through the brush and timber as they came across the hills to Oak Creek. Mr. Eggleston took up a homestead and built a house. He named the place Oak Dell. That place is now known as part of the Beech place. (1 mile So. of Tom Young, 95*)

Mr. Eggleston was a traveling dentist; he traveled through the small mining camps and communities in this vicinity practicing dentistry.

T. Witcher came to the west end of Fremont County in 1872 from Beaver Park where he had settled in 1867. He was one of the first cattlemen to settle here. He owned the ranch north of Cotopaxi that is still owned by his son Otis. (Gust ranch, 1995*)

Several families came into this district a short time later. Among these was the A. M. Smith family who came to Coaldale from Missouri in 1877. This was the father of W. H. and Charlie Smith who live in Coaldale. They bought the Billy Smith place from the four Camblin brothers-reputed horse thieves. Not having the money, Mr. Smith gave a note for the place. The brothers disappeared and they were never heard from again. (NOTE): The A. M. Smith mentioned above, located near the present town of Fountain in the 60's, but was chased out by the Indians, and returned to Missouri.

The Polson family came to Colorado in 1879. The place where they settled at Coaldale is now occupied by the family of one of their daughters, Mrs. Denick. (sp) (Floyd Porter, 1995*)

In 1873 the Phillips family came to the German settlement in the Wet Mountain Valley. Later they moved to Coaldale.

Also, north of Cotopaxi lived other cattlemen named Gross, Stultz, and Bernard. Some still call the creek which comes into the river from the north at Cotopaxi, Bernard Creek. The McCoy family moved to a place east of Cotopaxi in 1879.

Although they had no organized churches, early in the history of the community, traveling ministers had circuits through. The first one was John Stocks. He and his family lived in Hillside and his circuit went through the valley to Howard. This was in 1872.

The hunt for gold brought many people into this valley. Many rich strikes were being made in the mountain districts of Colorado in the 60's and 70's.

Probably the first as well as one of the most important of these prospectors was "Gold Tom". There seems to be some disagreement about what his name was; one authority says it was George Henry Thomas; others think his first name was Thomas. One story of him says that he was a partner of Bob Womack who made the big find in Cripple Creek, and it is a known fact that he spent a good bit of his time in Cripple Creek and other places prospecting. "Gold Tom" was the discoverer of the Cotopaxi mine and seems to have still owned it at the time of his death in 1882. He always carried his money and gold dust in a belt around his waist. People report having seen him open a small buckskin bag that would have held two cupfuls of gold dust and nuggets. A quarrel that probably started over the possession of a mine lead to the death of "Gold Tom". The immediate cause was the killing of a dog that belonged to a man named Meyers. A warning was sent out that he ("Gold Tom"*) was not to come to town again. When he did come in, trouble started. Meyer was sitting on the porch of the hotel, when someone told him that "Gold Tom" was looking for him. The store at that time was just across the street. As Meyer went in the front door of the hotel "Gold Tom" came out the front door of the store. He followed Meyer into the hotel. Inside he threw down one gun which he carried in his hand and drew his revolver. Meyer had run into the back room of the hotel. He couldn't get out of there and when Tom came in Meyer shot him. When the body was examined afterward, it was found that Tom's gun had jammed. Only $30 was found in money belt and none of the rest of his gold was ever found. He seems to have had no family except an aunt who lives in California. He is buried in the Cotopaxi cemetery, but the grave is not marked. From time to time since the death of "Gold Tom", some time has been put in by boys around town digging for his gold. It is supposed to be buried at the foot of a large rock just east of town about a half a mile. ("Gold Tom" Park,*1995)

Following the death of "Gold Tom", a rich Jew by the name of Sauteal (Saltiel,1995*) (There is some question concerning the spelling of this name) gained possession of the mine. He held it until it was sold to Gunnier (sic), an early cattleman of the district. The mill was built in 1920.

Many others have searched for valuable minerals in the vicinity, and the hills are honeycombed with the holes dug by these early prospectors. Mining today is largely confined to the mining of feldspar. This is used for building purposes, and for the making of crockery and glass.

The first quarry was opened by a man named Howard in 1886. This was the lime quarry four miles north of town. In 1889 Percy Gilman opened two granite quarries east and south of Cotopaxi. The granite quarry operated by Peter Noon, Ed Bowon and Charles McCoy was started in 1905. It was while loading stone on a freight car that Noon was killed by a falling derrick.

Lumbering was another early industry. Probably the first saw mill was the one owned by Clinton Biggs of Cañon City, the founder of Biggs Lumber Co. Much of the country on both sides of the river was heavily timbered. George Cooper reports that all there was, was a path through the brush. At that time no stream came down that gulch, and the surrounding territory has not been cleared.

In the early 70's a large forest fire swept the country south of the river, destroying a great deal of timber. It was this fire, however, that opened that section for settlement. The fire was started by a group of freighters who let their camp fire get out of control. Their camp was burned, but it is not known whether they escaped or not. When the camp site was found, there were several piles of flour which had been burned on the outside; the inside not having been hurt at all. Flour at this time was selling for as much as $1.00 a pound, freighted.

Among the first cattlemen were Bernard, Gross and T. Witcher; all of whom lived north of the river. South of the river most of the cattle belonged to William Beckwith. He came to the north end of the Wet Mountain Valley in 1870 with a large herd of Texas steers. Much of the fighting, shooting and other troubles started over the stealing of cattle. It is reported that three-fourths of the cattlemen got their start from the Beckwith herd. Stealing cattle from men with a heard too large to be accurately counted or taken care of was considered by some to be all right if they could get away with it. The crime was in getting caught rather than in the act itself.

The railroad went through Cotopaxi sometime in the winter of 1881. Before it had gotten this far, many of the ties used in building it were cut in the winter; and in the spring, when the river was high, they were floated down to Canon City and other points east. While the building was going on, many families sold meat to the construction gangs. Most of this was deer meat, some of it, however, sold by people not owning cattle, was beef sold as venison. At various times "detectives" were hired by the cattlemen to catch the rustlers. The result of getting caught was usually a ticket to the next world. It might be well to comment at this place that never has there been a jail of any kind in this part of Fremont County. Cañon City being the closest place to hold a prisoner.

Farming was not carried on very extensively. The main reason for this was of course that there was not much of a market for farm products. People raised much that they ate themselves, but very little besides this.

In 1882, 150 Jews were sent here from New York by a New York Aid society settled in Cotopaxi and south. They attempted to start an agricultural community this side of Hillside. They planned to dam the small creeks and streams for irrigation purposes and to raise sugar beets. The venture, however failed and the group remained only a few months. While here they built several of the first dwelling houses in Cotopaxi.

O. B. Carrol, brother of Mrs. Hendricks, owned the first store in Coaldale in the latter 70's and early 80's. Hart, a Jew, had the first store in Cotopaxi. In 1884, O. B. Carrol moved to Cotopaxi and bought the Cotopaxi store from Hart. He kept the Coaldale store for several years after this. The first store was located on the ground where the home of Mrs. Lois Bailey is now. This first store building was a two room structure that served as post office, store, dwelling and hotel when necessary. The second store that Hart built was a much more pretentious one and stood where the H. P. Mullins store stands now.

Other buildings in Cotopaxi when Mr. George Cooper came were the Hilton house that recently belongs to Dillingers, the two small houses that were moved together in the east end of town and are still standing. Part of the house where Mr. and Mrs. Cooper live was here early, too. These houses mentioned were nearly all built by the Jews the summer they were here. Hart also built the hotel which stands across the street from the Mullins store. (Where Glenn Mullins now lives, 1995*)

The first road was built through in 1876 and was for the freight wagons and stage coaches. As was said before, it followed in general the route of the Indian trail. The stops or stage barns were built to care for this group of travelers. At each stop horses were changed and all passengers got out for a short rest and for meals which were served at these places. The stage stops were not far apart because the rate at which the horses were driven did not allow for long runs. Good drivers were the ones that could get the most out of horses for the length of the run. The life of a stage horse was of course very short.

There was a stage barn as well as the first post office on Texas Creek above the present Coleman Place (Rosenthal, 1995*). The next stop after Texas Creek was near the Billy Smith place this side of Coaldale (Hidden Valley, 1995*). The next important stop was at Valley (Valle Bridge, 1995*). At one time there was a town of about one hundred people on the south side of the river at Valley, where the highway is now. The next barn above Valley was about at the county line. The next was at Cleora. Cleora was this side of Salida a short distance. It was first built when the railroads were having their fight over the right-of way in the gorge. The people who built Cleora were sympathizers with the Santa Fe. When the Denver and Rio Grande built their shops, they put them a few miles from Cleora and that was the end of Cleora. It has since burned down.

This stage road was very rough, and riding for the passengers was uncomfortable. The wheels of the wagon wore deep ruts into the road, and it was difficult for a wagon or a coach of any kind to turn. Sometimes, quarrels resulted over which should turn out, and occasionally they had collisions when neither of the rapidly moving vehicles would turn aside for the other to pass.

Stage fare was high. In 1879 when Mrs. Coleman and her small son came to Texas Creek, the fare was $3.00 from Canon City. It is now $.54 by bus or train. When the first railroad went into operation the fare was $.10 a mile.

The fight between the Denver and Rio Grande and the Santa Fe over the right-of-way through the Gorge was finally settled in 1880 and a narrow gauge track through to Leadville was finished in 1881. The branch line from Texas Creek to Westcliffe was built in 1898, after the Grape Creek road had been washed out. Until the branch line was built, the freighting to Silver Cliffe and Westcliffe was done by teams from Cotopaxi. Many large pieces of mine machinery went that way to the mines. Some of these were so large that it took as many as twenty horses to haul them.

During the years that this freighting was being done, Cotopaxi had about four or five hundred people living in it. There were two stores and three saloons. This was also the heyday for the cattle industry. As is to be expected there is always a certain amount of the "rough and ready" side of life in the development of a new country. Cotopaxi had more than its share of this it seems. Many stories came to light this side of life , as it seems to be one of the things that everybody know about and remembered. One that is authentic is the story of the mail robbery at Texas Creek in 1890. Four men held up the train by flagging it at the siding of Fernleaf one mile east of Cotopaxi. The men forced the fireman to open the mail compartment of the express car. They soon found that they had the wrong compartment because they had planned to open the one belonging to the express company rather than the mail. The story is that they did not touch anything in the mails but when two of them were sentenced they received sentences for robbing the United States mail.

The famous gunmen "Doc" Shores and Horn were hired by the railroad to catch these men. Shores got one of them, a man by the name of Burt Curtis. Horn trailed "Peg Leg" Aldrich for a long time and finally got him at Robbers Roost, Utah, where he was hiding. Both were brought back and sent to the pen for life. There were two other men, according to the story, but they were never found. Our story has it that their names were Boyd and Ward. Ward was never heard from again and the last anyone knew of Boyd he was in Salt Lake.

In tracing down the naming of the different towns we found many interesting stories. The creek known to us as Texas Creek was named by Joe Lamb and Nat Rich. They were taking a herd of long-horn Texas steers to California Gulch to be sold for meat. They camped on their way through Texas Creek, then an unnamed creek. During the night the herd was stampeded by a mountain lion. Some of the herd was never found and as they drove them away, they named the creek "Texas Creek".

The record says that the Texas Creek district was on the Squires place. One of the first teachers in this school was Mr. Coleman, who came here in 1879. Some of the children who attended this school were Lamb, McCormick and Lymon Hayden children. George Cooper taught this school in 1880. This is the school that was later known as the Hillside school. A school building in the same district was also built on the Lamb place on Texas Creek.

The first school at Coaldale was a little log cabin back of the place where Mrs. LeNoue now lives (Woody Shields, 1995*) This was built in 1878. The name of the first teacher is not known, but Mary Hayden was teaching there in 1880. There were no seats, just benches around the room. In 1880 a storm caused a flood, and the water entirely surrounded the school house so deep that the teacher (the same Miss Hayden) and the smaller children all had to be carried from the building. A very large and strong man, Frazee, by name, carried the teacher and children all out at one time. Some of the larger boys were able to wade to safety.

In 1878 three families living on Oak Creek hired a Miss Kirkendall to teach a small school there. She taught in a vacant house and boarded around with the three families whose children she taught: the Eggleston and Burroughs family. Seven children: Ernest, Warren, Willey, Frank, Clara, and Laura Eggleston and Ralph Burroughs attended this school. The next school in that vicinity was a private one taught by Mrs. W. K. Eggleston. This was taught in her own home in 1881. The children in this school were D. M., Laura, and Staymen Cooper, and Ernest, Elsie, Wallace and Warren Eggleston. There were no regular school buildings for either of these schools.

Most of these schools were log cabins. The seats were rude home-made benches, and the books were whatever they could get. Slates were not used extensively, but any available piece of paper was made to serve its purpose. In some instances the books belonging to one family were all the books those children used. The children were not graded according to their age or ability, but according to the books the family could afford them.

The Cotopaxi district, number 23, was organized July 29, 1882 out of "unorganized territory between districts 10 and 17". The description of the district as given in the county superintendent's office is of a territory to extend north of the river four miles, and from Fern Leaf Creek up the river to mile post 190. All the sides were to be parallel except the one that bordered on Fernleaf. The district was to extend up the river five miles.

Consolidation of districts 19, Texas Creek; and 23, Cotopaxi was finally brought about in 1917.

The year following consolidation there were three teachers in the Cotopaxi school. These three teachers had charge of seventy-six grade students and 17 high school. Ada Muhlback was the primary teacher, Jane McCormick (Mrs. Bert Blackford) was the upper grade teacher, and Hazel Penly taught the entire high school.

All but two of the high school were first year students. These two were sophomores who transferred from high school in Canon City.

At the time of consolidation, a new school building was built. It was a cement structure of four rooms. In 1928 three more rooms were added. Now we have a modern school building of seven rooms with our own electric light plant, a new auditorium-gymnasium, equipped with stage, dressing rooms, showers and a fully equipped kitchen.

NOTE:

The original paper was typed by Miss Dillinger, who was a teacher at Cotopaxi High School in the middle 1930's. She gathered this information from old-timers, located in and around the town of Cotopaxi; consolidated it, and typed this paper up in several copies.

The copy that is now held by the McNew family is a carbon copy, and the original and other copies are not found as yet, but it is thought that they were originated and distributed to interested persons in the West end of Fremont County.

This copy was typed and saved on computer disc on May 10, 1995 by Carol G. McNew, from the original carbon copy which was found in the effects of Sherman McNew. Kenneth McNew, father of Keith McNew (husband of Carol) was married to Ethel Storms, a granddaughter of George Cooper who is mentioned several times as a source of information in foregoing narrative.

This is the Cotopaxi D&RGWRR Depot which was built at the corner of County Road 12 and Plum Street. It was razed in the 1950's, as well as the section houses which stood beside it. Circa 1902

CHARCOAL WAS AN INDUSTRY FOR THE ENTIRE VALLEY IN 1900

Photo of the Coaldale kilns courtesy of Eleanor Fry as they look today

The McAllister Charcoal Kiln types were used throughout the region. The kilns were built from brick or native stone. The "Charcoal Burners", or owners of the business would buy wood from local

cutters, and carefully load the kilns so that they would burn very slowly. The remains of the charcoal kilns for which Coaldale was named. There were at least 5 of these kilns at this location, and these historic kilns are still visible next to the road on Hayden Creek, County Road 6, Coaldale.

Coaldale kilns when they were operating late 1800s and early 1900s. The name "Coaldale" was earned by the constant stream of black smoke emitted by these kilns, night and day while they were producing the charcoal.

FROM GRISWOLD'S HISTORY OF LEADVILLE

Quoting The Leadville Evening Chronicle, 5/14/1884:

•. .Among the first to introduce kilns was Mr. H. D. McAllister, of Utah under the patronage of the Germania or Utah Smelting Company, represented by Billing & Eilers. Their smelting works belong now to the Arkansas Valley Smelting Company. The burning of pit coal was then entirely abandoned and the charcoal industry of the Arkansas valley is now represented by the following set of kilns: . . .

There follows a list of 24 "Charcoal operations" throughout the area representing 166 kilns in production.: The story goes on:

Pine charcoal is sold at fourteen pounds to the bushel, pinion, eighteen pounds, 2,500 cubic inches in measurement makes also a bushel.

There were times when they received 16 to 18 cents per bushel. Some kilns produced up to 17,000 bushels a month.

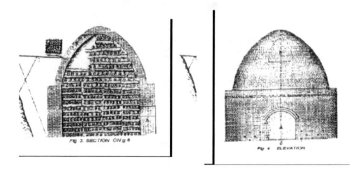

FIG 3. SECTION ON g 6

Fig 4   ELEVATION

HISTORY OF COTOPAXI, COLORADO AND ENVIRONS

By Carol McNew Revised: 3/10/01

ARCHEOLOGY OF THE AREA:

The area was occupied for thousands of years before the white man came by various native Americans. The "tribes" (so named by the white man) were lost in antiquity until the early 1700's when the explorers from the East came west and first encountered the various communities and their way of life.

The tribes which occupied this small area in Colorado were varied and intermixed, since we are at one of the crossroads of the Rocky Mountains.

The Ute and Apache Indians were the first to be identified with the Upper Arkansas River area in the early 1700's. In 1750, the Comanche and Apache shared the eastern plains and the Arkansas Valley. By 1820 the Comanche commanded the entire Eastern half of Colorado, while leaving the entire Western half to the warlike and fierce Ute tribes.

By 1820 the Arapaho and Cheyenne tribes infiltrated into the eastern part of Colorado pushing the Comanche into the most southeastern Corner, but they still shared the territory of Cotopaxi. By 1830 on, the Arapaho and Cheyenne continued to push their influence South, and controlled the entire eastern part of the Rocky Mountain area in Colorado.

Bands of Indians continued to roam the area until they were assigned land in the southwestern section of Colorado and moved there forcibly.   There were tales of Indians approaching homesteaders in various parts of the West end up until the 1920's.

The era of French traders and trappers spurred by expeditions led by LaSalle and other French explorers kicked off the occupation by white men after the initial Spanish expeditions in the early 1600's. The Mallet brothers, Peter and Paul crossed over into the Arkansas drainage in 1739. These early mountain men trapped beaver, hunted elk and deer, and were friends and allies with the remaining Indian tribes taking wives and living with them during the winters while trapping for furs.

The Arkansas Valley was Spanish South of the River and French North of the river until 1800, when it was ceded to France. Three years later the United States purchased the territory from France

Sieur Bernard La Harpe, a map maker, named the Arkansas River in 1718.

Zebulon Pike led his men meanderingly along the Arkansas River and through Cotopaxi (we presume) in 1806.

The country was laced with cattle trails, deer trails and various other primitive paths and byways. There are also many "prospect holes" throughout the area, which were dug by men looking for the riches of Silver, gold and copper. The discovery of gold, silver, lead and other precious metals in the high mountains spurred the development of transportation, which could provide a way to haul supplies to the mines and ore from them.

There were numerous "Road Companies" incorporated in the years that followed (see Colorado Corporations on the internet). The road to Leadville from Canon City was long and difficult. The most effective way to move large volumes of either supplies or ore was the railroads. In 1880, through many harrowing wars and legal battles, the Denver and Rio Grande Western Railroad reached Leadville and affected the lives of everyone along the path of the narrow gauge rails which it followed.

The freight roads to the mines in Leadville were started in Canon City, traveling up through Oak Creek Grade across Webster Park. It followed Copper Gulch to Road Gulch (modern names, of course) and across the hills to Pleasant Valley never reaching the river until it crossed it at Vallie Bridge. The side roads to Texas Creek and Cotopaxi were developed to supply those towns and to haul produce, etc. from those places to Canon City. There was a road company incorporated to build the road from Coaldale across

Hayden Pass into the Wet Mountain Valley. That road is still available for 4 wheel drive vehicles.

The railroad required thousands of ties to lay the tracks and these were produced and hauled to the river by the tie hacks who built log cabins throughout the hills to live in while they cut ties to ship. The ties were shipped by wagon or floated on the river down to the end of the railroad bed. There are many old disintegrated cabins throughout the hills around Cotopaxi, which attest to the tenacity of these "tie cutters".

In 1872 the first twenty-five thousand ties floated on the river; they were added to at each town, then were sent to feed the railroad builders from Fort Dodge. By the time the ties reached Canon City their number had been increased considerably along the way and 100,000 ties were being floated past that city. A major industry developed from the railroad's need for ties.

Meanwhile, back at the ranch in Cotopaxi the Prospector, Henry Thomas, has been laying claim to a Mine which he developed up Mine Gulch just Northwest of Cotopaxi about ¼ mile. He named the mine the Cotopaxi Lode because it reminded him of a similar place in Ecuador. He named the mountain in which it was located "Volcano Mountain".

He lived in a small log cabin about ½ mile down river from Cotopaxi, which is now known as Gold Tom Park. He had a placer claim there and permission from the railroad to prospect along the tracks. There is still a large stone with the word "Gold" engraved in it with an arrow. The story of the murder of Gold Tom by George Myers (in June of 1884) is available in many articles written by Vic Miller for the Pueblo Chieftain. Henry Thomas is buried in Greenwood Pioneer Cemetery in Canon City.

In 1880, Silver Cliff just 25 miles South of Cotopaxi was booming with the silver discovery there (by 1881 a population estimate of 6,000 to 16,000). This provided another commercial opportunity for anyone wishing to cut mine props and ties for rails into and out of the mines.

Cotopaxi had freight outfits, stage barn, depot, saloon, a general store, post office and hotels to accommodate the influx of miners and others intent on getting rich quick. The roads to Silver Cliff, Leadville, Fairplay and other camps all went through this valley because of the railroad.

Emmanuel Saltiel, a businessman and entrepreneur filed a claim for the Cotopaxi Silver Lode at the base of Volcano Mountain in June of 1879. This claim evidently was a "deal" between Saltiel and Thomas. He also filed a claim for property adjacent to the Arkansas River containing 160 acres. This is the property upon which he built his home which has also been referred to as Saltiel's "hotel". This also included the land lying beside the Atchison, Topeka and Santa Fe Railroad tracks. The water rights for this land were filed on by Mr. Hylton in 1871.

The town (or the railroad) installed a low-sided wooden bridge across the river for access, and a granite quarry South of the town shipped many tons of dress ed granite to various building sites throughout Colorado. Pete Noon was the last known owner of this quarry, and he was killed by a boom as they were loading blocks of granite. (in 1925) The buildings to which this stone was shipped included Denver City Hall, State Office Bldg., The U.S. Post Office and the Continental Oil Building.

The McCoy family is famous throughout the United States for their murderous natures and felonious intent. There were many stories published about them, from Victor Miller's "Old West" tales to the stories in the New York Times written by hacks that enhanced the story to their liking.

There is a rumor that the former Mrs. T. Witcher actually hired the McCoy gang to murder her husband. That, of course, will never be proved.

The McCoy cabin and corrals are preserved for posterity at the East end of Red Gulch north of Cotopaxi and is now owned by John Caldwell of Salida. The original cabin has been modernized somewhat, but the area is still reminiscent of a "hole in the wall" hideout for desperados. The saloon which Charley McCoy ran for many years (as well as a store at one time) was moved to the back lot of Cotopaxi in 1970 and there is disintegrated.

The town continued to be a hub for commerce for the outlying ranchers and industries, quarries and freighters. The ranchers furnished beef for the mining camps and railroad workers. Looking at the census figures from 1880 and 1900 many of the homes included boarders who were listed as miners or Day Laborers or farm hands. The picture taken in 1890 from the South side of the river shows the Saltiel house, the hotel/boarding house, the Hart/Carroll store and home next to it, the depot and perhaps 5 more dwellings. There is another picture, gleaned from the Colorado Historical Library #X-7403, which shows the town with many tents, a few small residences, the depot, Saltiel's house (greatly expanded from what we know is there today.)

Cotopaxi opened it's first Post Office in June of 1880 with Frank W. Wood as postmaster. The railroad was the postal delivery system for Cotopaxi.

The town continued to expand and change as the homestead act came into play and an influx of from 30 to 100 "nesters" flocked to the high mountain valleys and streams to claim from 160 to 640 acres of land for themselves.

The mining industry was not quite done, though. In 1909, the Copperfield Consolidated Copper Co. was incorporated with general offices in Denver and mine office in Cotopaxi, Colorado. The mines were 10 miles north of Cotopaxi and the prospectus shows a veritable community with many fine pictures of the working miners and the hand drawn engineering reports of the wonderful lode of copper which they were going to extract and ship.

The Copperfield mine lasted only 5 years. The buildings were abandoned and torn down in 1914 by John O. Ireland and used to build his homestead house in Nesterville.

The Cotopaxi Mine also had a resurgence of life when a gentleman by the name of Augustus R. Gumaer came into possession of the mine. He shipped ore from the mine until his death and his brother inherited the mine. He sold it to a gentleman by the name of James Locke of Canon City.

In the year 1920 at the Cotopaxi Mine, a 100-ton concentrating mill was erected by Nebraska promoters, the mill being engineered and built by Peter Young, who was brought into the area for that purpose. It operated only a short time, and was again sold to Donalver Brothers and H. P. Mullins of Cotopaxi.

One other industry, which affected the entire valley, was the charcoal kilns which ate Pinon wood by the ton and which denuded the hills around all the settlements as evidenced by some of the older pictures. Charcoal was shipped to the CF&I Iron mills in Pueblo as well as limestone from the many quarries throughout the area. The railroad was the main shipping means.

The first school in Cotopaxi was a structure built on the original Saltiel claim just North of the railroad. It housed several classes from 1st to 12th grades and was constructed sometime between 1884 and 1886. The District was #23 and was visited by the Superintendent of schools Mr. Jacob H. Freeman in 1886. The gentleman had to travel up Copper Gulch and across to Oak Grove Creek to reach Cotopaxi and the Howard district.

Previous to this and even during the period that Cotopaxi school was in existence several schools were provided by "subscription" meaning the teachers were housed by parents and taught wherever sufficient room and materials were available. This was the case in Nesterville, Hillside and other locations in the district.

In January of 1915 John Ireland asked to detach portions of Dist. #10 and #23 in the north part of these districts and form a new district. This would have been the Nesterville district. Denied.

In June 1917 Districts #10, Texas Creek and #23, Cotopaxi were voted to become Consolidated district #41.

Homesteaders in the Nesterville area gathered in Mrs. Imogene Forshey's house to study the bible they did not have an organized church to attend.

There were two schools built in Nesterville: The Nesterville School and the Yellow Pine School. Both of these buildings were moved to Cotopaxi when the schoolhouse burned in 1939 for additional school rooms while the new school was being built. The children from the area were bussed to Cotopaxi in a Kissel bus until the vehicle with hard tires could no longer negotiate the steep, rough road.

NOTE: The text of this history of Cotopaxi was given as a lecture to the Western Fremont County Historical Society in March of 2001 by Carol McNew.

A very beautiful building in Howard for the children to go to school. On Howard Creek, the old Howard School. *(Ross Collection)*

WHITEHORN
1860——1925

Fremont County has it's fair share of ghost towns, but one of the most remote and forgotten is the community of Whitehorn in the far Northwest corner of the county.

Whitehorn was founded on the same principles as most of the towns in this area: minerals, including gold, silver, copper, zinc and lead. The prospects of fabulous wealth evidently created grandiose dreams by the influx of more than 200 families at the height (1900).

The town boasted saloons, grocery store, stage station and blacksmith facilities for the population. The school at Whitehorn was initiated by a petition from 60 of the residents, respectfully asking the attention of the then County Superintendent B. G. Woodford. The petition asked for a school district be established and directors appointed thereto. The stationery used to proffer this plea was from the Miner's Restaurant, James Brooks, proprietor.

The census for 1900 shows over 200 people and the census for 1910 shows almost as many occupants.

Whitehorn had a newspaper "The Whitehorn News", which enthusiastically covered all the happenings in this frontier town. The first death is recorded on Feb. 10, 1899 being the son of Mr. and Mrs. D. D. Babb who burial was in the cemetery established "on the mesa just east of town".

The advertisement for A. L. Whitehorn, "U.S. Deputy, Mineral Surveyor, etc" located on upper Main Street is evidence of the gentleman's industrious nature.

The town plat of Whitehorn which shows the various mining patents as well as a very ambitious street, lot and alley design. One of the few towns in Western Fremont County that was so platted.

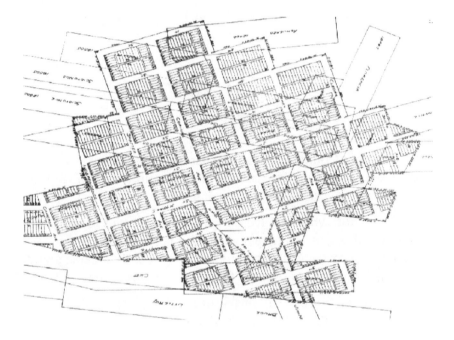

COPPERFIELD
1900————1913

The promoters of Copperfield extolled its riches to the world in a prospectus published in 1909. The capitalization of 750,000 shares at a Par Value of $10.00 each was expected to finance a mining operation that would return millions to those astute enough to hand over their money.

Copperfield was located 10 miles North of Cotopaxi on the Red Gulch road where an outcropping of copper ore was found by prospectors, filed on, and then sold to promoters from Denver. They constructed a company store, boarding house, and cabins and houses for the mine foremen.

The mine buildings were placed along the East Side of Red Gulch at spaced intervals and each mine given a name (see 2nd page over). The mining engineer, Robert S. Billings, ME stated in glowing terms the probability of the mines being comparable to "Cripple Creek, which is only 20 miles away."

Mr. J. B. Conger, Pres.; Mr. E. G. Bettis, Vice Pres.; Dr. Arthur W. Miller, Sec & Treas.,; and Mr. E. H. Cook, Gen'l Super. Were accorded beautiful portraiture as the "Active Management of the "Copperfield Consolidated".

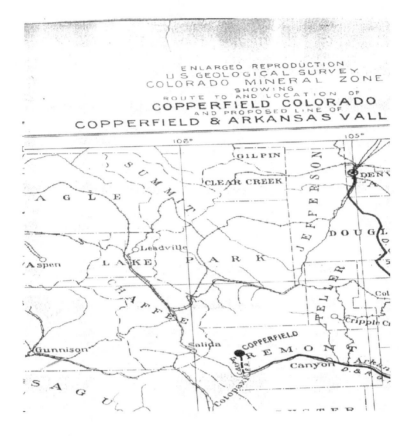

ENLARGED REPRODUCTION
U S GEOLOGICAL SURVEY
COLORADO MINERAL ZONE
SHOWING
ROUTE TO AND LOCATION OF
COPPERFIELD COLORADO
AND PROPOSED LINE OF
COPPERFIELD & ARKANSAS VALL

HIGH HOPES

"The promise of Copperfield is a long life of ore bodies succeeding ore bodies and for generations."

"There is no industry that pays more, greater, and more certain dividends, and no business more important, except the single industry of agriculture, than is mining, and of the dividend paying properties none are more sure, more unfailing, none pay higher rates than the producers of copper. Hence the inducement to open the vast riches that Copperfield assures; hence the value of the investment in Copperfield shares."

"The promise of Copperfield is unexcelled and every indication is that veins are unusually large and unusually rich in copper, and at present depth there are few equal showings in the United States."

The **Copperfield Pioneer,** the newspaper of the town of Copperfield, and of the company, so touted this bonanza in 1909. Note the addition of the Copperfield and Arkansas Valley R.R. to accommodate hauling ore for the mines.

TIE HACKERS-PROSPECTORS-CHARCOAL BURNERS

The 1860's to 1880's were a busy time in Western Fremont County. There was a lot of activity surrounding the small villages.

The timber on the slopes and valleys of the area fell to the axes and saws of various groups, mainly tie hackers for the railroad. This activity sent up to 100,000 logs down the river during flood time during the years the railroad was building towards the mining camps.

The charcoal burners were skilled men in the making of charcoal for smelters and the iron works in Pueblo. The piñon pine forests were thick throughout the foothills below the mountains. There were kilns in every community. Texas Creek, Cotopaxi, Coaldale and Howard still have remnants of the kilns that were used to turn out thousands of tons of charcoal.

The prospectors were a group of men who managed to cover every inch of the terrain looking for possible mineral outcrops. There are thousands of small "prospect holes" which can be seen today on ridges up and down the valley. There were even a few which had enough ore to pay wages. The paying mines turned out to be lowly limestone, marble and bentonite. The CF&I Steel Mills in Pueblo developed resources throughout the region for their use.

TEXAS CREEK TO HILLSIDE

Texas Creek is the light at the end of the long tunnel of the Grand Canyon of the Arkansas. There were bright spots along the way with hardy souls who lived within the fastness either serving the railroad or possible mining interests.

The open areas around Texas Creek were welcomed and there were a Post Office, a restaurant, boarding house and the ever-present railroad depot and agent's home. There is little there now to suggest more than one a family operation. There are two derelict buildings on the North side of the river which attest to the possible golden days. The gulch running north from the river is also Texas Creek (North) and the creek coming from the South is almost never dry and is the Texas Creek we refer to.

State Highway 69 runs directly South from Texas Creek 10 miles to the small village of Hillside. (and on to Westcliffe) This entire area has been farmed and ranched from early times when people first entered into this valley because of the constant flow of water which issues from the Sangre de Cristo Range to the West.

Many ranches and small farms are tucked into the piñon hills. The road was one of the original freighting highways from Road Gulch to County Road 1A then on to Hayden (Coaldale), and thence up County Road 45 to Wellsville.

COTOPAXI MINE

The copper mine located within Volcano Mountain, on mine gulch northwest of Cotopaxi has had a long and varied history. The mine was a magnet for other prospectors to try their luck around the area. The copper ore is found in many outcroppings in the hills.

Henry Thomas actually located the Cotopaxi Mine and named it. He eventually sold it (or lost it) to Emanuel Saltiel who is infamous as the Russian Jewish importer to acquire cheap labor for the mine.

The mine has passed through many hands since 1882.

In 1919 Peter Young, an engineer, was hired to construct a mill at the Cotopaxi mine. This structure was demolished a few years later.

BOILERS FOR STEAM:

The mine operation at the Cotopaxi Mine used powerFurnished by the huge boilers moved in when the large

Processing plant was built in 1920.These coal/wood fired boilers were moved in and Bricked up by the company. Construction behind The boiler is the processing mill framework.

CASH CROP FROM THE NESTERVILLE RANCH

The homesteaders found virgin, fertile ground to grow their crops in the Nesterville community. There was an abundance of water in the spring, because of the high elevation (9,000 ft. plus) the snow melted slow, and the springs ran for a long time.

The cash crop for most were potatoes. In the picture we see John Ireland with a load of potatoes headed for Cotopaxi and the railroad. They would be loaded on a car and shipped to the penitentiary or other retail outlets in Cañon City. The other crops of oats, barley, hay and lettuce gave the people the cash to buy the necessities like coffee, sugar and flour at the local store.

Only two mules were needed on the trip down the hill to Cotopaxi or Cañon City but the trip back up the steep road needed four animals to pull the load up the hill. There were regular "spring" stops where the men and animals could drink on their way back to Nesterville.

The road up "Red Hill" is a 6% grade when it leaves Red Gulch to go into the Long Gulch drainage. The elevation at Cotopaxi is 6400, the elevation at Nesterville (the Ireland place) was 9,500 feet; thus the climb of 3100 feet in 20 miles.

Thhreshing—John Ireland's"

The back of this photo has the above legend. The crop is not explained, but presume it is oats or barley.

The machine was probably the itinerant threshing machine and crew run by Otis Witcher in 1915 through 1920s. The threshing machine was pulled all over Fremont and Custer County to thresh the various grain crops grown by the farmers and ranchers of the area. Only one person is identified in this picture, C.E. Ahart was part of the neighbors helping the Ireland's get in their crop. He is identified as one of the men standing to the left in front of the machine.

John and Edith Ireland homestead house in Nesterville, built from Copperfield building lumber

COTOPAXI

The road into Cotopaxi from the Texas Creek-Hillside connection came in from the South. The creek was so choked with oak brush that it was named Oak Grove Creek. The freighters on their way to Leadville avoided coming down the three miles and 750 feet into Cotopaxi if their horses were fresh enough they could make the next five miles into Pleasant Valley. (Circa 1875)

Two of the businessmen of Cotopaxi formed a road company and built the road from Cotopaxi to Coaldale along the river. This improved the freight hauling so much that freighters then came North into Cotopaxi and on up the river road.

Cotopaxi boasted many businesses in the late 1800s and early 1900s. The railroad brought civilization and the ability to ship the produce of the farms, the miner's ore and the granite, limestone and charcoal produced for the smelters and the railroad, itself.

The town was built slowly. The picture we have of early 1902 show many tents and temporary shelters. The school was an integral part of this little village; the Cotopaxi Mine and Railroad were big employers. Let's not forget the charcoal kilns, limestone kilns and ranchers who were part of the economic picture.

Cotopaxi, 1902

NEW SCHOOL AT COTOPAXI"—1890

The new school was built with three rooms originally and two rooms were added later. The average school year lasted from 6 months to 9 months and the children were expected to help out at home when necessary. The graduating class of 1924 had three seniors.

This building burned to the ground in 1939. Only the foundation was saved and converted into the cafeteria.

1877 —- ——— 1899

Fremont County was divided to create Custer County in the 1870s. The Post Offices which were established throughout the area after the division were:

Galena	Pleasant Valley
Hayden Creek	Coaldale (Hendricks)
Cotopaxi	Parkdale
Ford Juniper	Palmer (late Hayden)
Titusville	Texas
Wellsville	Howard (Pleasant Valley)
Grape	Hillside (late Texas)
Hendricks (late Palmer)	Texas Creek (Ford)
Whitehorn	

Post offices now available in Western Fremont County are:

Hillside, Cotopaxi, Coaldale and Howard. Texas Creek is served by Cotopaxi P.O. and Swissvale and Wellsville are served out of Salida.

BARNES CITY AND TUBERCULOSIS CAMP

1902— - - - - - - - ——— 1920

There was a gentleman from England who came into the valley in early 1900s to promote a mining enterprise and town located three miles South of the road on Hayden Creek. His name was Noah E. Barnes and he brought his family; wife N.E., daughters Ada and May, Fred and Mrs. Fred, and a grandson named Fred Jr..

The occupation listed for Mr. Barnes was "mine promoter, Copper & Gold" Owns the land, no mortgage." His son Fred, was the Mining Company Treasurer.

The village of Barnes City sprung up with dance hall, saloon, homes to live in and invitations to partake in striking it rich with the mining claims showing excellent gold possibilities. The parties and picnics promoted by the owners of Barnes City were attended by many of the citizens in the area.

Today, there is no trace of this enterprise. The homes were built without foundations and only smoothed squares of ground are visible where once a thriving community lived.

GYPSUM AND RHYOLITE

1890- - - - - - - - - - - - - 1996

The Gypsum mine at Coaldale was started "before I can remember," a quote by Stella Denek in her interview by Bullard & Gillespie. The wagon road which was used to haul the ore to the railroad had ruts so deep that it was almost unusable by other vehicles. She also tells the story of the mule, "Kate": She was used to help the teams pull the heavy loads through the boggy ground the last quarter mile to the river. The mule would then be turned loose to return to her waiting station at the school for the next load.

The flux mine across the river at Coaldale was owned by CF&I and at one time had tracks which ran straight down the mountain for the ore cars. The loaded car going down would pull the empty car back up the mountain. A trace of this operation now is the "W" showing the trail up to the mine.

A short drive up Kerr Gulch there was a quarry, where huge slabs of RYOLITE were mined and shipped for buildings throughout the state. These slabs were unique in that the process used could produce larger pieces than most other quarrying cutting devices. More pictures of this quarry are available online at the

Denver Public Library Western Division.

The vision of the Sangre de Cristo Mountains as you enter the Coaldale Valley from the East and the wonder continues on around the horizon.

HAYDEN, PALMER, HENDRICKS AND COALDALE

1860

The entrance into the Pleasant Valley from the Grand Canyon of the Arkansas is so breathtakingly beautiful that people stop on the highway and jump out to take pictures of the awesome sight they behold.

The majestic peaks of the central Sangre De Cristo Range in all its glory are visible. The open valley and colorful foothills are the stuff calendar pictures are made of; the ranch houses and livestock contribute to the scene.

The small village of Coaldale had many changes of name during its 150-year history. The original settlers (Hayden) (Palmer), then the homesteaders (Hendricks) and eventually the charcoal industry (Coaldale) all had a hand in naming the area.

At the time Coaldale was first settled the main road from the East ran next to the foothills away from the river and only came to the river at the West end of the valley where appropriately enough, another settlement was established named Vallie. This was a good fording place and later a bridge was built across the river.

Once a great many homes and public buildings stood. The area is privately owned and is not available to public viewing.

Up the road (South) was another gathering of shacks and tents constructed by the necessities of life for many tuberculosis patients who were sent to this area to recover from the disease. Old timers remember that people would just move into whatever shelter was available and live there for some time. (Probably not through the winter since they are very severe that close to the mountains).

The tuberculosis cure in the pure mountain air was not always certain but it brought in many of the settlers to this area. This particular "community" up the Hayden Creek Road was only one of many places that people attempted to cure the disease.

There is no trace of this particular settlement, either. There are private residences now in the general area. However, the beautiful Hayden Creek still runs along cheerfully through this wonderful little valley and its beginning high in the range was developed for a road to the San Luis Valley in the early days probably used by the Indians for a passage, also.

The Hayden Creek Pass is four-wheel drive only in good weather but worth the trip if you are ever in the area in mid-summer.

VALLIE

Yes, it is spelled correctly. The crossing of the main freighting road at the West end of the Coaldale valley was a natural place for a settlement to spring up. The railroad had a depot, a boarding house and probably section crew shacks. There were some homes and one that was built from cement block was only recently razed.

An orchard was planted and remained producing apples up into the late 1980s. The railroad boarding house was operated by Orpha Dees wife of George Dees, the Section Foreman. Boarders at the time of the 1900 Census were: Fred Greve, Mike Maher, Peter Clark, and William Carroll.

The water tank at Vallie and the settlement are long gone. The BLM has built a boat ramp for rafting, restrooms and picnic areas next to the river just across the bridge.

The county road is #45 which continues on up the river to the town of Howard.

KerrGulch Quarry Early 1900s

HOWARD

The town of **Howard** was established before the coming of the railroad because of the lush meadows and available water in the creeks. The farming/ranching community also was boosted by the charcoal kilns, tie cutting, sawmills, mining ventures etc.

The railroad brought economic prosperity to the area and the town was centered around it on the north side of the river, although now many businesses and homes line Highway 50 which travels on the south side of the town.

The town boasted an "Opera House" at one time and built the community building for events and the Grange to hold meetings. There was a baseball team organized and the Great American Sport was enjoyed up and down the valley.

"Howard Hall" as it was for many years- now replaced with a new Hall and this one has been torn down.

Howard, Colorado in early days. The town hasn't changed much except for paved roads and vehicles.

Howard was a focus point for shipments of limestone quarried from the hills of Calcite, just three miles south. There were also several charcoal kilns placed next to the tracks (and which were bulldozed by the railroad in 1980).

CALCITE
1902—1929

The company town of Calcite was based on the premise of economics for the company, which happened to be CF&I Steel Corp. The workers were from many foreign countries, attracted by the mining profession. Only a few of the original families still remain in the Howard area.

Company housing for all the employees, a company store, school, and recreation hall were amenities provided by CF& I.

The D&RGRR built a spur to accommodate the shipping of the precious Limestone to Pueblo steel mill. This trestle was part of the complex that existed up until 1930.

Limestone Kiln built at Calcite to process the limestone on site

SWISSVALE AND WELLSVILLE

FAR WEST FREMONT COUNTY

The river road winds its way westward into the amazing "S" curves that precede entrance into Swissvale. There is another BLM camping/boat launch area previous to starting into the "S" curve portion. This area is called Rincon. The red sandstone outcroppings that march down from the hills on either side of the river create a changing panorama of formations.

The village Swissvale is blessed with fairly level ground before the banks drop off into the river. The population of this area has increased 1000 fold in the past 20 years with subdivision of the land on both sides of the river.

The few businesses in Swissvale are on the highway: a taxidermy, a resort (now closed) and a liquor store.

The original highway from Howard to Salida traveled on the North side of the river and remains of it can be seen all along the road. This is still a usable road and many fishermen and gold panners use this road for access to the north side of the river. Construction in the summer of 2001 improved the roadbed considerably at the narrows.

The limestone kiln near the Wellsville turn off from Highway 50. This kiln is next to the railroad track just ½ mile West of the bridge, and was one of many such that were dotted throughout Western Fremont County for the processing of limestone.

WELLSVILLE

The "resort town" of Wellsville was a favorite spa for folks in the late 1800s and early 1900s. The wonderful hot springs which bubble to the surface throughout this area were captured and a beautiful pool and changing rooms were built. The swimming pool was a popular place for folks to go.

The Wellsville community also had a baseball field that was put to use every weekend and ball teams from throughout the valley and Salida would converge for the great American Pastime. All is gone, now.

Wellsville also shipped quick lime which was produced in the lime kilns from the limestone in the outcroppings of the area.

The present day manufacturing of "Marble" by the U. S. Marble Company produces marble-like material from ground ores.

The rock formations in this area are spectacular. Notice in the picture there is no road on the South side of the river (where Highway 50 now is).

The swimming pool at Wellsville, built before Highway 50 was constructed on the South side of the river.

Hunting camp in the early 1900's. One of many pictures now in the McNew Collection, Coaldale, CO.

THANKS TO ALL THESE FOLKS FOR THEIR INSPIRATION

• Archeology of Colorado by E. Steve Cassells, Johnson Books, Boulder1983

Colorado South of the Border, Ralph C. Taylor, Sage Books, Denver, 1963

Trappers to Tourists by Rosemae Wells Campbell, CenturyOne Press, 1972

Claim Deed by Emmanuel Saltiel describing the Cotopaxi Lode, at the base of Volcano   Mountain dated June 20, 1879

The Pueblo Chieftain, May 30, 1965, article by Victor Miller

Wet Mountain Valley, by Gayle Turk, Little London Press, 1975

The Cotopaxi Colony, by Flora Jane Satt, University of Colorado, 1950

Old West magazine, Vol. 6, #4, published 1970

Newsletter of the Fremont-Custer Historical Society, Vol. II No. 3, May 1973

From Slate to "Apple" Fremont County School Days published by the Fremont County Extension Homemakers, compiled by Marie Green, Margaret Sanders, Carol Seal, and Silvia Allen, 1986

Linda Goddard and Rita Aten for Howard Historical Days, Calcite

Interviews by Bullard and Gillespie, Alice (Weeks) Munson, 1986

THANKS TO YOU, TOO:

USGS, Phone call 12/18 "Public Domain map", McAllister kiln drawing
Denver Public Library, Western History Division, Coy
Canon City Public Library Local History Center
Marque Cooper, Denver
Kenneth McNew family
McNew family collection
William Reich
Oscar Ireland collection,
Lanell Bullard and Joann Gillespie
Witcher collection, Local History Center, Canon City
Eleanor Fry, Pueblo, CO
Western Fremont County Historical Society
Thomas A. Young